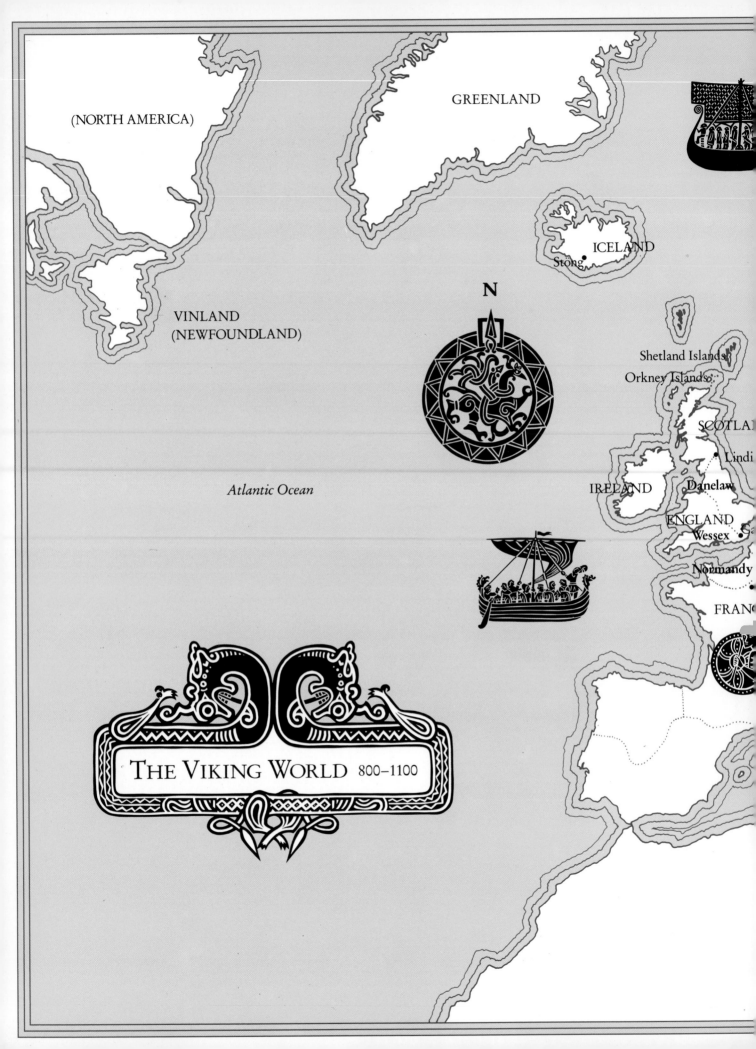

(NORTH AMERICA)

GREENLAND

ICELAND
Stöng

VINLAND
(NEWFOUNDLAND)

N

Shetland Islands
Orkney Islands

SCOTLA

Lindi

IRELAND          Danelaw

Atlantic Ocean

ENGLAND
Wessex

Normandy

FRANC

THE VIKING WORLD 800–1100

Arctic Ocean

VISU (SIBERIA)

NORWAY

SWEDEN

DENMARK

deby

Hamburg

Refic

Novgorod

(RUSSIA)

Smolensk

(POLAND)

Kiev

River Dneiper

Caspian Sea

River Rhine

(GERMANY)

OLY ROMAN

EMPIRE

(ITALY)

Rome

Black Sea

Byzantium

BYZANTINE EMPIRE

Mediterranean Sea

MUSLIM ARAB EMPIRE

# THE
# VIKINGS

LIVING HISTORY

# THE
# VIKINGS

JOHN D. CLARE, Editor

GULLIVER BOOKS

HARCOURT BRACE & COMPANY    SAN DIEGO   NEW YORK   LONDON

First U.S. edition 1992

First published in Great Britain in 1991 by The Bodley Head
Children's Books, an imprint of The Random Century Group Ltd
Created by Roxby Paintbox Co. Ltd

*Gulliver Books* is a registered trademark
of Harcourt Brace & Company.

Library of Congress Cataloging-in-Publication Data
The Vikings/edited by John Clare.
p.      cm. — (Living history)
Includes index.
"Gulliver Books."
Summary: Describes the daily life and customs of the Vikings and
examines their many roles as farmers, traders, explorers, raiders,
colonizers, and mercenaries.
ISBN 0-15-200512-9
ISBN 0-15-201309-1 (pbk.)
1. Vikings — Juvenile literature. [1. Vikings.] I. Clare, John,
1952–   . II. Series: Living history (San Diego, Calif.)
DL65.V565   1992
948 — dc20   91-24146

**Director of Photography**      Tymn Lyntell
**Photography**      Charles Best
**Art Director**      Dalia Hartman
**Production Manager**      Fiona Nicholson
**Visualization/Systems Operator**      Antony Parks
**Typesetting**      Thompson Type, San Diego, California
**Reproduction**      F. E. Burman Ltd
                     Columbia Offset Ltd
                     Dalim Computer Graphic Systems U.K. Ltd
                     J. Film Process Ltd
                     Trademasters Ltd

Printed and bound in China

A    B    C    D    E
A    B    C    D    E    (pbk.)

ACKNOWLEDGMENTS

**Advisor:** Dr. Dominic Tweddle, York Archaeological Trust. **Make-up:**
Alex Cawdron, Sarah Packham. **Models:** Chris Lovell, Neville Smith.
**Old Norse language advisor:** Dr. Richard Perkins. **Picture research:**
Valerie Tongue. **Props:** Mark Roberts. **Set design and building:** Art FX
Associates. **Set dresser:** Jennifer Nevill. **Viking coordinator:**
Phil Bertham.

Additional photographs: Julian Bajzert, pp. 1–5; Icelandic Photo and
Press Service, pp. 32–33; Spectrum Colour Library, pp. 8–9; Swedish
Tourist Board, pp. 30–31; Werner Foreman Archive: p. 6 bottom right
(Thfodminjasafn, Iceland), 46–47, 63 (Statens Historiska, Sweden);
Zefa Picture Library, pp. 12–13, 40–41.

# Contents

# The Vikings Are Coming!

The people who lived in the northern part of Europe between A.D. 800 and 1100 were known as Norsemen, Northmen, or Danes. They were famous and feared as pirates and raiders. In later years they came to be known as Vikings, a name derived from a Norse word for pirate, *vikingr*. The Vikings, however, were not just warriors. They were also remarkable explorers, settlers, traders, and craftsmen. They lived in a time of great possibilities and great change.

## THE VIKING WORLD

The Vikings shared a language called Old Norse, a religion, and many customs, but they were not a unified nation. Their loyalty belonged first to their clan (family) and then to their local community. Each year these communities held assemblies called Things, at which all freemen voted for leaders and laws. Gradually, in the years after 800, three important Viking kingdoms — Denmark, Norway, and Sweden — began to take shape. New Viking communities were also established in Iceland and Greenland. But the Vikings never had one central government.

By contrast, in A.D. 800 much of the rest of Europe was dominated by three powerful empires. The Holy Roman Empire included France, Italy, and Germany, all ruled by the Emperor Charlemagne. The Muslim Arab Empire controlled most of Spain and the lands to the south and southeast of the Mediterranean Sea, while the wealthy Byzantine Empire controlled the land between the Mediterranean and the Black Sea.

## RELIGION AND SACRIFICE

By 1100 the Vikings had converted to Christianity, but in the ninth and tenth centuries they believed in many gods. Odin, the god of poetry, battle, and death, was the most powerful of all; the Vikings believed he was the gods' father or leader. Myths describe him riding an eight-legged horse across the skies, accompanied by wolves. His symbol is the raven. Odin ruled over Valhalla ("the Hall of the Chosen"), the Viking heaven. When a Viking died in battle, a supernatural warrior maiden called a Valkyrie brought him to Valhalla, where he fought all day and feasted all night.

Thor, ruler of thunder and sky, was the most popular god. Many Vikings wore

lucky charms shaped like the hammer he swung to make thunder. Thor supported law and justice, and in his honor the Icelandic national assembly (the Althing) always opened on a Thursday — Thor's day.

Frey, the god of harvest, ensured good crops, and his sister, Freya, the goddess of love, gave large families. Their father was Njord, the god of wealth, fishing, and sailing.

To honor their gods, the Vikings offered

sacrifices. Often conducted by a chieftain-priest called a *gothi*, ceremonies were held in a temple or a sacred place outside. Vikings could offer anything of value — silver and gold, boats, weapons, statues, clothing, animals, and even human beings. Most sacrificial objects were buried or thrown into a river or bog; sacrificed animals were eaten.

The greatest sacrifice was to give up a son. When a war against neighboring Vikings was going badly, Earl Hakon, ruler of Norway from 965 to 995, promised to sacrifice his young son, Erling. The tide of battle turned immediately, and Hakon gave the boy to his servant to be put to death. When the Vikings converted to Christianity, the custom of making sacrifices died out.

TRAVEL AND TRADE

By the eighth century A.D. the Vikings' Scandinavian ancestors had trade links with western and eastern Europe, Byzantium, and even China and India. They found the southerners eager to buy northern falcons; marten, beaver, and squirrel fur; walrus ivory; high-grade iron; and amber.

Archaeologists have uncovered many treasure troves of coins and jewelry that indicate that Scandinavia in general and Sweden in particular were very wealthy. We know the century before A.D. 800 was a time of warfare partly because those who buried treasure often did not survive to collect it. During this early period, Scandinavians developed a fighting spirit and pirate tactics, improved their ships' design, and became skilled sailors and navigators. Travel and raiding became part of the Scandinavian way of life.

Nobody knows what inspired the Vikings to begin making raids on towns and monasteries in the rest of Europe. Some historians believe it was their improved ship design, others think that changes in the weather made sea travel easier, and still others think that a population explosion en-

couraged the Vikings to look for new lands. In any case, by A.D. 800, King Godfred of Denmark felt powerful enough to declare war on the Holy Roman Empire. He attacked and destroyed Reric, a Slavic trading town, and moved its merchants to Hedeby in Denmark — thereby increasing his country's wealth through trade. Three centuries of Viking raids, travel, and conquest followed.

# Viking Homelands

There were three classes of people in Viking society: the jarls, the bóndis, and the thralls. The jarls, or earls, were chieftains, military leaders, and sometimes priests. The bóndis, or freemen, were farmers or merchants. The thralls were slaves.

A jarl or a wealthy bóndi would own a *bær* (farmstead) and about 30 thralls. He or she could also hire poorer freemen to work for pay. The thralls, who were either born to slavery or captured in battle, had to wear white coats and crop their hair short. They did much of the heavy labor on the farm. A hardworking thrall might become a *bryti* (farm steward) or *deigja* (housekeeper). Some farmers let their thralls work on other farms for pay or share in the profits from raids. In this way, some thralls earned enough to buy freedom. But a thrall's life was hard. Viking law permitted a jarl or bóndi to beat his thralls to death, provided he publicly announced what he'd done on the same day.

On a small farm the whole family shared the work. Children helped with the hay and grain crops and looked after the livestock, mostly cattle, sheep, and goats. But Vikings did not value skill in farming as highly as skill in fighting. One Viking story praises the aggressive behavior of a boy named Grettir, who killed his family's geese rather than look after them.

---

*The main building of the* bær *is the wooden longhouse. Its roof and walls are covered with straw. In summer, children play on the soft roof, and goats try to climb up to eat the straw. Sometimes farmers waterproof their roofs with tar. The* bær *also includes a byre (cow house), barns, stables, and a bathhouse. The best place for a* bær *is at the foot of high grassy slopes. In summer farmers graze livestock on the mountain pastures. Wealthy farmers also move their families to a* shieling, *a small summerhouse.*

9

# Inside the Longhouse

Archaeologists have excavated a typical Viking longhouse at Stöng, Iceland. The entrance, through a single door, led to the hall, or main room. Along each side of the hall ran a bank of earth that served as a sleeping place at night and a bench by day. There were three more rooms: a workroom for the women, a food storage room, and a room that might have been for cold storage.

Most doors, pillars, seats, and wall panels in the longhouse were made of intricately carved and painted wood. Houses did not have glass windows, but Vikings often cut a small *skjár* (opening) into the gable end and stretched a transparent *skjall* (the membrane that covers a newborn calf) over it. The *skjall* let in a small amount of light.

Near the center of the hall lay a clay-covered hearthstone, where a fire burned all day. Smoke escaped through a *ljóri*, or hole, in the roof. If the house was attacked, the *ljóri* was a convenient escape hatch. The fire provided heat for cooking and was the only source of warmth. Some halls had iron candle holders, but in most the fire was the only source of light after dark.

*A Viking wife runs the household. She supervises the female thralls, who cook, spin, and weave. She often works with them, manufacturing the woolen cloth she sells to traders, or in summer helping with dairy work or the harvest. At her side she carries the keys to household chests that contain her family's valuables — ornate weapons, jewelry, and coins. When her husband leaves home to go raiding, he publicly hands over his own keys as a sign that she is now in charge of the house and farm.*

## Winter Activities

In Viking times the Scandinavian climate was warmer than it is today. Winters, nevertheless, were harsh, so the farmer and his family left the *shieling*, the small mountain home where they spent the summer, and returned to the *bær*.

On October 14, the Vikings made the winter sacrifice, to ask the gods for mild weather. From January 12 to 14 they held a second ceremony, the Yule sacrifice, for which the Viking priests, or *gothi*s, sacrificed a "forgiveness boar" and asked Frey, the fertility god, for prosperity and peace.

Though Viking women worked year round, for men winter was largely a time for leisure, repairing tools and weapons, and building battle skills. One Viking poet describes how the sons of jarls and freemen learned to "shoot arrows, ride on horseback, hunt with hounds, brandish swords, and do feats of swimming." Men challenged

each other to climb up a sheer rock face or jump off a cliff, maintaining their fitness and readiness for battle. They wrestled, juggled with knives, and played games, including a board game called *hnefatafl* and a ball game called *knattleikr*.

Violence was a part of the Vikings' recreation, just as it was of the rest of their life. They enjoyed watching stallions fight until one killed the other. In swimming competitions, contestants tried to drown their opponents. Wrestling, *knattleikr*, and even *hnefatafl* could end in a fight or death.

*Clockwise, from bottom left: the Vikings play board games such as merils (similar to checkers) and* hnefatafl *(the board and pieces resemble those used for chess, but the rules are different).*

*Using a technique called tablet weaving, women make braids and decorative edgings for clothes and linens.*

*Children play with dolls, strap on bone-bladed skates for ice skating, and play a bat-and-ball game called kingy bats.*

*Using wooden swords, boys prepare for battle by practicing swordplay. Their fathers wrestle to increase their strength.*

# Shipbuilding

When winter ended, in April, the Vikings offered Odin a victory sacrifice for success in the summer raids. Then the men began to build or repair their boats.

The Vikings loved their boats. They built and sailed many kinds, including fishing boats and cargo vessels, but most beloved were their longships, which they used to wage war. Most boats were oak and had the same basic form, though cargo vessels were broader and heavier and had more storage

room than warships, which could be up to 180 feet (55 meters) long. The *Long Serpent,* a famous longship that belonged to King Olaf Tryggvason of Norway, was 120 feet (37 meters) long. A more ordinary longship was 76 feet (23 meters) long.

To enemies, Viking longships were terrifying. They were astonishingly swift and easy to maneuver because they had a rudder. Longships were decorated with carvings, weather vanes, and gold-plated designs, and the prows were often carved to look like dragon heads. A longship's striped, square sails could look like a drag-

on's wings, the oars like its legs. Vikings gave their warships names such as *Raven of the Wind* and *Ocean-striding Bison*.

*Tools used to build the hulls of the ships include an ax (far left) for trimming the strakes (side-planks), an adze (above left) for shaping curves, and a molding iron (above) for planing wood. When they are finished, the lower strakes are only 1 inch (2.5 centimeters) thick.*

*The shipwrights below have already positioned the lower strakes to overlap and made the ship watertight by filling the cracks with moss or animal hair covered in tar. Now they are adding the ship's internal supports, or crossbeams. At the prow and the stern the beams will be tied on with leather thongs to give the ship flexibility.*

## A Viking Raid

Accounts of Viking raids vary widely. A 12th-century English monk named Simeon of Durham, whose monastery in Lindisfarne had been raided in A.D. 793, wrote of the Vikings' invincibility, blood-thirstiness, and brutality. The Vikings, he says, trampled on altars, looted precious relics, and drowned the monks.

*The Saga of the Men of Orkney*, written by Scandinavians around the year 1200, presents the raids in a different light. It describes how Svein, a jarl who keeps a large household, sows and harvests his crops in the summertime — and, during spring and autumn, sails south to go raiding. To the Vikings, Svein seemed generous and brave.

Monasteries were the Vikings' favorite target because much of a country's wealth was to be found in their treasure rooms.

The Vikings did have laws that forbade them to attack traders, farmers, women, or men already involved in a fight, but these laws were not always followed. Raiding was simply part of a Viking's life, and in a Viking's eyes, the more successful the raider, the better a Viking he was.

The great Icelandic hero Egil Skalla-grimsson was an ideal Viking. When a rich farmer imprisoned him, Egil managed to escape, taking the farmer's silver with him. But as he ran, Egil realized that he was behaving like a common thief — so he returned. Only after killing his enemies did Egil carry his treasure away with a clear conscience.

*Speed and surprise are the key elements of a successful Viking raid, and longships are perfectly designed for sudden attacks. The warriors sail right onto the beach, carry out the raid, load the ship with captives and booty, then escape before a defense can be organized.*

## The Raven Banner

A fter A.D. 800, Viking raids increased in number. A French monk wrote that raiders "carried everywhere the fury of fire and sword, gave up the people to death and captivity, devastated all the monasteries, and left them filled with terror."

Gradually, the raids became an invasion. Raiders settled on the Orkney and Shetland islands north of Scotland, where they enslaved the natives. Others built forts in Ireland and attacked Irish monasteries. In 844, Vikings established themselves on islands off the coast of France, and in 851 they spent the winter in England for the first time. In 865, a number of Danes banded together to form the Great Heathen Host. For 30 years they terrorized western Europe. Flying a banner depicting a raven, they conquered northern and eastern England, forming a territory known as the Danelaw.

When the Host pressed farther south into Wessex, the English King Alfred hid in the marshes with a small guerrilla band and mounted a series of successful counterattacks on the Danish invaders. By May 878 he had forced the Vikings to surrender and won a temporary peace. The Danes retreated and settled farther east, and 30 Danish leaders were baptized as Christians.

*It is January 878. Facing Alfred and his band, the Vikings form a shield wall and fly their raven banner, which they believe will bring them victory.*

*Soon, the battle will become a free-for-all; 840 Danes will be killed, and the famous banner will be captured. Inset left: A group of Viking soldiers take up a pig's snout formation to defend a narrow gap.*

## Tribute and Danegeld

In 880, some members of the Great Heathen Host broke into Wessex again, then left England to raid northern France and Belgium. Other members invaded Germany, then crossed back into England.

The Vikings often demanded a tribute — a sort of bribe to make them go away — known as danegeld. The raiders divided the wealth equally and took it home; in Sweden alone, archaeologists have discovered over 30,000 early English coins — more than have been found in England. During the ninth century the French handed over a total of 685 pounds (311 kilograms) of gold and 43,042 pounds (19,524 kilograms) of silver. In 911, King Charles of France gave part of his kingdom to a Danish Viking called Rollo the Fat in return for Rollo's promise to drive away the other Vikings. This area came to be called Normandy, because the "north men" lived there.

Each new round of attacks brought higher demands for tribute. In 1012 the Vikings demanded 48,000 pounds (21,772 kilograms) of silver from the English, as well as a ransom for the Archbishop of Canterbury, whom they were holding captive. When the Vikings did not get the extra money, they pelted him to death with bones.

Four years later Cnut of Denmark conquered all of England and collected 82,500 pounds (37,422 kilograms) of silver. He then declared himself king of all England.

*Monks and a young landowner ensure the safety of their district by paying tribute.*

# Weapons and Warriors

The most feared Vikings were the berserkers — warriors, either men or women, who fought furiously in battle. Some historians think they chewed on fly agaric (a type of toadstool that causes a hypnotic rage). Berserkers believed they could not be wounded, and they fought either naked or wearing animal skins. When they became battle-crazed they ground their teeth together and bit the edges of their shields. Sometimes, if the fury came on while they feasted, they rushed out to wrestle with boulders until it wore off. Vikings respected the berserkers but they also recognized that the berserkers were dangerous.

*The Vikings, such as this warrior (top), Rus trader (center), and bowman (bottom), treasure their weapons and battle garments, giving them poetic names.*
*Below: Someone wealthy enough to own a byrnie (a coat of mail) might call it Odin's Shirt or Battle-cloak.*
*Right, top to bottom: Helmets — which do not have horns — have names such as War Boar. Weapons include small daggers, a spear, an ax (Wolf of the Wound), and a bow and arrows. Swords like these might be named Odin's Flame or Viper of the Enemy. The best swords are imported from Germany and inlaid with the signature of Ulfberht the blacksmith.*
*Viking arrows have specially designed flights (above, far right) and heads (bottom center) for every task from killing men to catching fish.*

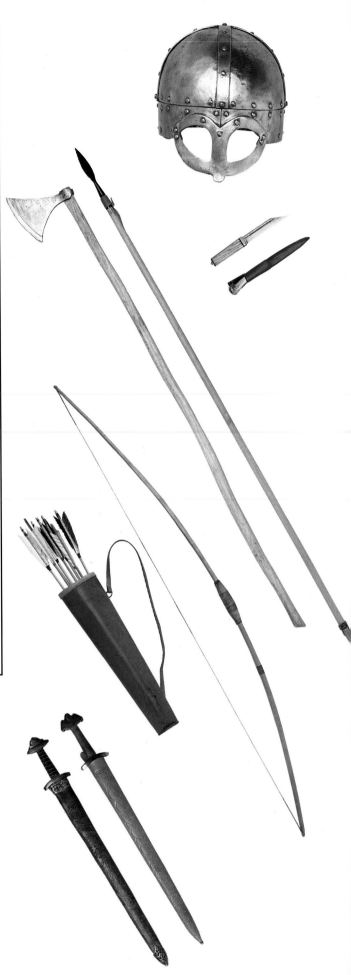

# Raising an Army

The sagas tell us that when a Viking leader needed to raise an army, he sent out a messenger carrying an iron arrow. In Norway and Denmark this messenger traveled around *skipreitha* (ship districts), each of which was commanded by a *thegn* (war leader). Every man who saw the arrow, including thralls, had to join the local war leader's ship within five days, combed, washed, and fed — or be outlawed. A widow had to send her male servants. In theory, therefore, a Viking army was made up of troop levies (men who had been drafted), each led by a *thegn* or *gothi*.

The warriors of the great raiding armies may have been raised in other ways, how-

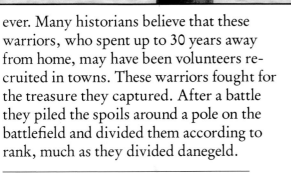

ever. Many historians believe that these warriors, who spent up to 30 years away from home, may have been volunteers recruited in towns. These warriors fought for the treasure they captured. After a battle they piled the spoils around a pole on the battlefield and divided them according to rank, much as they divided danegeld.

*Below: Crews vary in number depending on the size of a ship, but usually there are about 30 men. Each rowing place is called a room, and the size of a ship is measured by the number of its rooms. The warriors sit on chests in which they store their weapons and clothes.*
*Right: The levies bring equipment for the voyage — a sail, weapons, rope, a cauldron, sacks of grain, and water barrels, as well as deer pelts and drinking horns.*
*Left: A rich Viking brings a byrnie and other personal possessions, including a decorated drinking horn, a comb, fire-lighting equipment, and dice made from antlers.*

## Burial Ceremonies

Funeral ceremonies varied. When a Viking warrior died a ceremony called *nábjargir* was often performed. A relative closed the body's eyes and mouth and sealed the nostrils. Then an old woman known as the Angel of Death washed the dead man's hands and face, combed his hair, and dressed him in his best clothes.

A dead man or woman could be either buried or cremated. Most Vikings who chose burial were laid into the ground without a coffin, their bodies resting in a bent position. Some graves were left unmarked, but others were covered with a raised burial mound or outlined by a pile of stones. In some places the body was cut up and taken to different parts of the country. An important chieftain might be buried in a wooden grave house or a grave ship.

Most people were buried with all the things they believed they would need in the

cock. Women were buried with their cooking, weaving, and embroidery equipment. Occasionally, a warrior's wife or thrall chose to accompany him to the afterlife by dying in his funeral pyre or being buried alive in his grave.

afterlife. Grave goods might include beer and food, weapons, jewelry, clothing, horses, and dogs — sometimes even a pea-

*Dressed in his best clothes and resting in a coffin lined with warm furs, a Viking warrior lies waiting for burial in a grave ship (inset). A thrall, who believes that she will be the warrior's consort in Valhalla, has agreed to be buried with her master.*

## Feasting and Storytelling

Feasting was a favorite Viking activity — particularly during the long, idle winters. On the first day of a feast the jarl or bóndi woman of the house ordered several servants to hang tapestries in the hall and to set out the tables and benches. Other servants spread straw on the floor and brought in the *skapker*s (beer barrels).

The guests arrived wearing their best jewels and finest wool and linen clothes. The guests of honor sat with the hosts by the high-seat pillars in the center of the room. Sometimes the guests drew lots to decide where they would sit. If a young man repeatedly drew a place next to the same girl, he was expected to marry her.

Viking hosts had to offer their guests the best food they could afford. Some favorites were meat, spit roasted, boiled, baked, or

raw; sausages, made from lard, blood, and meat; and fish, dried, pickled, smoked, salted, or raw. Vikings ate very few vegetables, but they always had plenty of bread, cheese, and porridge. They seasoned their food with garlic, mustard, horseradish, and spices imported from the East.

The hosts' daughters served ale and imported wine. Once they had filled a drinking horn it could not be put down until it was empty. Feasts lasted several days, and Vikings often became quite drunk. Sometimes rival warriors attacked the longhouse while the occupants were too drunk to react.

---

*Poetry and storytelling are two important* íthróttir *(skills). While the hosts and guests of honor sit between the decorated high-seat pillars, a poet, or* skáld, *tells a story about Odin. Stories of the gods and heroes are rarely written down. Instead, the Vikings pass them from generation to generation by word of mouth.*

# Writing in Runes

Like wrestling, swimming, and storytelling, writing was considered by Vikings to be a special skill, or one of the *íthróttir.* The Viking alphabet was called the *futhark* after its first six sounds: *f, u, th, a, r,* and *k*.

ᚠᚢᚦᚨᚱᚲ ᚺᚾᛁᚨ ᛊᛏᛒᛗᛚᛦ

f u th a r k : h n i a   s : t b m l R

It was made up of letters called runes. Vikings did not have paper, so they carved their runes on bone, wood, and stone. The

runes were made with straight lines so that they were easy to carve.

Rune stones, often decorated with black, red, blue, and white paint, were erected to establish an heir's right to an inheritance or to record the adventures of those who, for example, "journeyed far for gold" or "shared out the spoils of war in Frisia." Some record misdeeds — for instance, "Höskuld lied to his oath-sworn friend." Others are memorials to loved ones: "Birging, rest in peace, loved by me, Vag."

Runes were useful for everyday writing such as labeling a sword with its owner's name or keeping merchant's records, but the Vikings believed they had magical properties as well. Someone who knew runes could use them to blunt enemies' weapons, break chains, or make one person fall in love with another. Vikings also thought runes would cure illnesses, guard against witches, and protect men in battle or at sea.

Wherever they went, the Vikings left rune graffiti on rocks and buildings. The messages show how far the Vikings traveled and how many kinds of people knew runes. "These runes were carved by the man most skilled in runes in the western ocean," boasted a Viking sheltering inside an ancient burial mound on an Orkney island.

*Top left: Although there are several runic alphabets, the Danish version is the most common.*
*Center left: The runes inscribed on this sword blade may give it magic powers. The small bone and wooden markers can be tied to objects to prove ownership.*
*Above: A craftsman uses a pointed hammer to inscribe a rune stone in memory of a Viking woman.*
*Right: The Lingsberg rune stone in Sweden is a memorial to Halvdan, an 11th-century Viking. The cross at the top of the stone shows that he was a Christian, but the carvings of dragons and other beasts are remnants of earlier Viking beliefs.*

# Voyagers to Iceland

The Vikings reached Iceland sometime around A.D. 860, and in 874 two Norwegian brothers set out to colonize the island. With them went 3,400 settlers. Most of the settlers were Scandinavian, though some were Irish slaves.

The emigrants sailed in cargo ships called *knörrs*. They took animals, seeds, looms, whetstones, and bellows, as well as the high-seat pillars from their longhouses and the metal parts of tools such as axes, shovels, and swords, cooking cauldrons, and moldboards for plows.

Voyages over the open sea were hazardous. No one knows exactly how the Vikings navigated. They probably sailed near shore and steered by landmarks, but when there was no land in sight they navigated by latitude, starting at one point and following the sun in a straight line. They steered with a large oar, called a steerboard, on the right side of the ship. Our word "starboard" comes from "steerboard." It took courage to cross the ocean in a boat only 76 feet (23 meters) long. Waves could reach 100 feet (30 meters), and the Vikings were often shipwrecked.

On board the *knörrs* the emigrants ate dried fish, salted meat, buttermilk, and hard rye bread. They stored freshwater rations in large casks. It was too dangerous to light a fire on board, so they did not cook their food. Each passenger had a leather sleeping bag for protection against the weather, but conditions were cramped and often cold.

*A Viking widow, Auth the Deep-minded, emigrates to Iceland with her household. When land is sighted, she orders her men to throw the high-seat pillars overboard. Wherever they wash ashore the settlers will build their new home.*

# Things and Althings

The Icelandic settlers brought Viking ideas about government with them to their new land. They divided Iceland into districts and established a Thing (assembly) in each. Local Things met every spring and autumn to set taxes, make sure every man had the correct weapons, and investigate murders. In Denmark, Norway, and Sweden, Things also elected kings, but the Icelanders were wary of giving individual leaders too much power and chose not to have kings. Instead, each summer they held a national assembly called the Althing. Gathering around the Lögberg ("Law Rock"), the Icelanders decided together how to run their country.

In all the Viking countries, every jarl or bóndi was expected to take part in the local Thing, though men living alone and widows had to go only if the Thing had been called to hold a murder trial or choose a king. Each Thing lasted about a week and ended in a ceremony called *vápnatak* ("weapon-shaking"), at which the Vikings clashed their weapons together to show they agreed with the Thing's decisions.

The Thing had no power to enforce its decisions, so a Viking was bound to the law by his sense of duty. Community spirit was strong. The Icelanders, for example, were grouped in *hreppr*, districts of around 20 farmers, that organized the yearly sheep roundup, cared for the poor, and aided families who lost their homes or crops. The Vikings believed it was a man's duty to plow old people's fields before he plowed his own.

*A jarl addresses a local Thing. People come to discuss local government and legal matters as well as to trade, play games, and exchange gossip.*

# Duel

To resolve disagreements, a Viking could challenge his opponent or enemy to a duel fought with swords, spears, or axes. The Vikings believed the person in the right would win. Such duels were trials by ordeal—if an accused man won the fight, he was innocent. Other duels were fought when a woman declared she would marry the man who won her in combat; these duels were fought to the death.

Berserkers sometimes made a living from dueling contests. A berserker could travel the country challenging men to fight, demanding a prize when he won. Many men, knowing they could not win, simply handed over their property, or even their wives, without a fight.

*Níth* (mockery) and insults were enough to spark a duel, or even a feud that would last for generations. Family ties were close, and a quarrel with one person often led to a feud with his or her entire family, including uncles, aunts, and cousins. Most feuds developed because a member of one family had killed a member of another. Duels and feuds were a common part of Viking life, but they caused many problems. During his reign, King Cnut of Denmark (996–1035) made dueling, as well as berserker behavior, illegal.

---

*A hólmganga duel has strict rules. A referee with an ax watches as the men fight on a cloak ten feet (three meters) square. If either man steps off the cloak he is nithing (a coward). Each man is allowed three shields. If either man's blood falls on the cloak, he may withdraw from the fight. At the end the man with the most wounds pays his opponent an agreed amount in silver. If he dies, however, all his property goes to the winner, so hólmganga duels are usually fought to the death.*

## Viking Law

---

The Vikings' legal system was well developed, and to make sure everybody knew the laws, an elected *lögman* (lawman) read them to the crowd at each Thing.

Several laws protected women's rights. Women were allowed to own property, and it remained theirs even after marriage. They had some say in the choice of a husband. A man could not kiss a woman who was not his wife, or even sing love songs to her. If he beat his wife, she could demand a divorce.

If 10 persons accused an adult of a major crime, they had to take their case to the *lögrétta* (law court) held on the Sunday of each Thing. The Vikings assumed an accused person was guilty unless he could prove his innocence. An accused man might swear by the gods on a priest's ring, call 12 men to swear to his innocence, or undertake an or-

deal such as walking over red-hot iron. An accused woman might pick holy stones out of a cauldron of boiling water. The Vikings believed that the gods would keep the innocent person safe. The role of the Thing was to state what law applied in each case and to decide on a punishment.

Vikings had no prisons. If found guilty, a criminal had to pay a fine. Small-time thieves were shaved, tarred, and made to run the gauntlet between two rows of people throwing stones. A murderer had to pay *wergild,* blood money, to his victim's family. For the worst crimes, the criminal was outlawed. An outlaw owned no property, and no one was allowed to help him. Anybody could kill him without punishment.

*The accused is brought before a panel of neighbors and given the chance to prove his innocence. If he cannot prove it, they will decide on a punishment and then clash their weapons together to show that they all agree.*

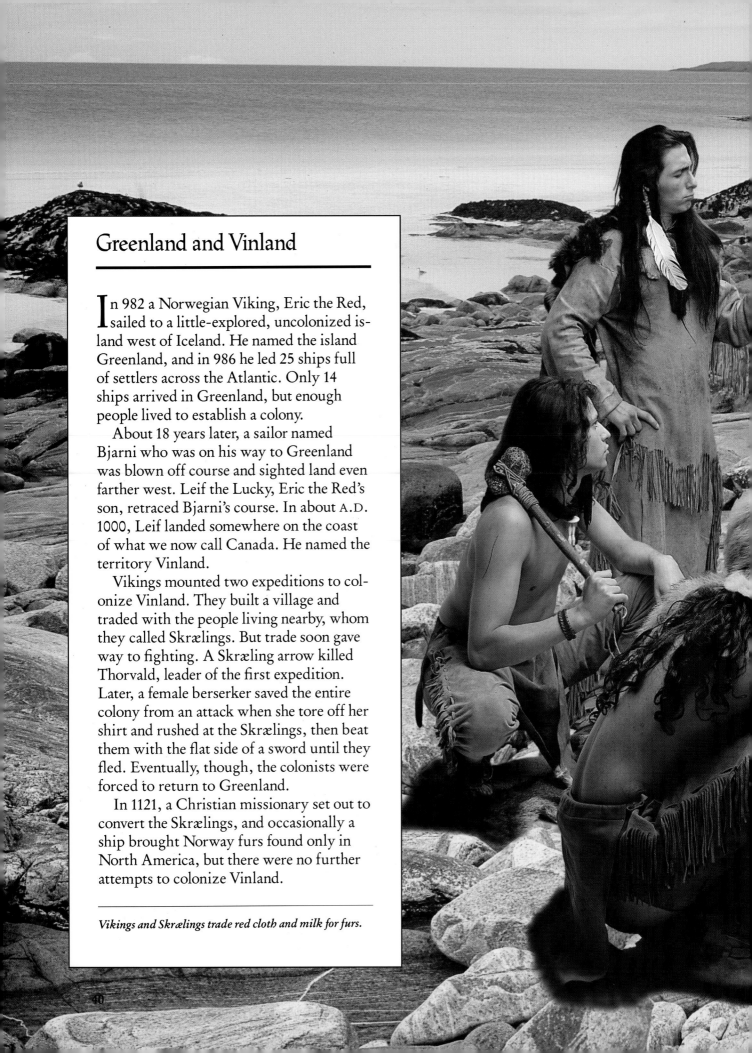

# Greenland and Vinland

In 982 a Norwegian Viking, Eric the Red, sailed to a little-explored, uncolonized island west of Iceland. He named the island Greenland, and in 986 he led 25 ships full of settlers across the Atlantic. Only 14 ships arrived in Greenland, but enough people lived to establish a colony.

About 18 years later, a sailor named Bjarni who was on his way to Greenland was blown off course and sighted land even farther west. Leif the Lucky, Eric the Red's son, retraced Bjarni's course. In about A.D. 1000, Leif landed somewhere on the coast of what we now call Canada. He named the territory Vinland.

Vikings mounted two expeditions to colonize Vinland. They built a village and traded with the people living nearby, whom they called Skrælings. But trade soon gave way to fighting. A Skræling arrow killed Thorvald, leader of the first expedition. Later, a female berserker saved the entire colony from an attack when she tore off her shirt and rushed at the Skrælings, then beat them with the flat side of a sword until they fled. Eventually, though, the colonists were forced to return to Greenland.

In 1121, a Christian missionary set out to convert the Skrælings, and occasionally a ship brought Norway furs found only in North America, but there were no further attempts to colonize Vinland.

*Vikings and Skrælings trade red cloth and milk for furs.*

# Down the Dnieper

At the beginning of the ninth century, Swedish and Danish traders sailed down the River Dnieper into what is now called Russia and the Ukraine. The local Slav tribes called these travelers the Rus, from the Old Norse word for "route."

The Rus conquered several cities, including Kiev, Novgorod, and Smolensk, and used them as bases for raids and trading. In Novgorod they established an annual fair that attracted merchants from all over Scandinavia. Some of the Rus, looking for silk and lizard skins, rode camels toward India and China. They also traveled to a land they called Visu (possibly Siberia), where the winter days were only one hour long. Local people would not meet them face-to-face, so the Rus left their goods on the ground. When they returned they found furs beside their wares — they could keep the furs or take their own goods back.

Other Rus sailed to the Black Sea and attacked Byzantium (present-day Istanbul), which they called Miklagard — "the great city." They could not conquer the city, but they did win the right to trade there, as long as they entered in unarmed groups of 50 men or fewer.

Many of the Vikings' customers in Byzantium, Russia, and Scandinavia were from the powerful Muslim Empire. In 922, Ibn Fadlan, a Muslim diplomat, met the Rus on the Volga river. He described them as tall, red-haired, tattooed, and "the filthiest of God's creatures." He seems to have been both fascinated and horrified by them.

*Rus traders carry their boat overland to avoid one of the seven rapids on the River Dnieper. They slide the oars through the oar holes and use them to lift the boat.*

## Trading Slaves

The Rus lived on the tribute they demanded from the Slav tribes, including furs and human beings they sold as slaves. They could either sell their slaves in Scandinavia or sail 1,500 miles (2,400 kilometers) downriver to the markets of Byzantium.

When a Rus trader reached a town he moored his boat near the marketplace and built a large warehouse to store his goods, including slaves. Then he made an offering of bread, meat, and leeks to a Viking idol — a wooden post carved with a human face.

Slave traders were the richest of all merchants. A wealthy trader could offer his customers their choice of a dozen slaves. Sometimes he might have English monks and others who had been kidnapped in Europe, but most slaves were Slav peasants — in fact, the word "slave" comes from "Slav."

A goat or a fine rain-cloak might be exchanged for a young boy. A woman might cost a mark (200 grams of silver). A Viking called Hoskuld once paid 3 marks for a girl of 15 who was "beautiful of face." Later, she told him she was an Irish princess.

The Church tried to stop the slave trade because it did not want rich Arab traders buying Christians and taking them back to the Muslim Arab Empire. One day, when Bishop Rimbert of Hamburg rode past a line of slaves in Hedeby, Denmark, one of the women shouted to him that she was a nun and sang psalms to prove it. The bishop immediately bought her from the merchant, although it cost him his horse and saddle and he had to walk back home.

*A priest and a slave trader haggle over the price of four Christians who have been kidnapped and enslaved. The trader weighs the priest's silver on his scales and tries to persuade him to pay more.*

## The Varangian Guard

I n the tenth century the Rus and the leaders of the Byzantine Empire signed a
treaty allowing the Rus to fight as mercenaries for the emperor of Byzantium. These
men, known in Byzantium as Varangians,
fought on the frontiers and in the provinces
of the empire, and in return they were
given lodging, food, regular pay, and a
share of the booty won in battles. They also
served in the emperor's bodyguard, which

came to be known as the Varangian Guard. They considered themselves the best of all Vikings — thus, the best fighters in the world.

Harald Hardrada (1015–1066) was the bravest, fiercest, and most famous of all guardsmen. When he had a chance to become king of Norway, however, he decided to leave Byzantium. The empress tried to keep him from going; she even threw him in jail to make him stay. But Harald escaped, and he and his men sailed for Scandinavia. As they left the city, the empress ordered an iron chain to be stretched across the harbor mouth. Harald had his men stand in the back of the boat while he sailed it up onto the chain, then made them run to the prow. The boat tipped forward, slid over the chain, and escaped.

*Pestered by traders, Varangian guards stand side by side with Byzantine soldiers protecting the walls of Byzantium. Though they are proud of their loyalty to the emperor, the elite guardsmen despise the local people and treat them roughly.*

# Battle at Sea

A round the time the Varangian Guard took shape, a similar band of mercenaries called the Jomsvikings formed in Denmark. Though their fortress at Jomsborg has never been found, sagas say it had a harbor big enough for 300 longships.

Only unmarried men between the ages of 18 and 30 could join the Jomsvikings,

and they swore to treat their comrades like brothers. They always avenged their brothers' deaths and put all treasure into a common fund. A Jomsviking could never flee from battle — one warrior kept firing his arrows even after both his feet had been cut off.

Jomsviking warriors were known for their strength and bravery, so it is not surprising that they fought in two of the greatest naval battles of the Viking age. In 990

they fought in the Battle of Hjörungavag with the king of Denmark when he tried to invade Norway, and in 1100 they joined forces with the kings of Denmark and Sweden against Norway's King Olaf Tryggvason in the Battle of Svold. Despite the Jomsvikings' skill and bravery, however, in both battles they fought on the losing side.

*At the start of a naval battle the warriors blow horns, taunt the enemy, lower the sails, and raise the standard.*

*They hang wooden hurdles over the sides of their boats to protect the strakes. Warriors from both sides pull the ships together with grappling irons and tie them to make a floating platform. Men board the enemy ships and fight their way along, driving their opponents back inch by inch. The captain stands in the stern, where his bodyguard forms a shield wall to protect him. The air is full of the sounds of taunts, oaths, and horn blasts.*

*The bravest warriors are always positioned in the front of the ship, where the most important fighting takes place. Berserkers are not always useful in sea battles. Sometimes they become so enraged that they forget where they are and charge right off the ship into the sea.*

## At the Wharfside

During the Viking age, Scandinavian towns grew and became centers for manufacturing and trade. Farm families and villages that had once grown only enough food for their own needs now tried to produce a surplus to sell to the towns to support the growing populations. An in-creasing number of trade ships brought foreign goods to the ports.

The Vikings imported such luxuries as glassware, jewelry, Rhineland pottery, French wines, German swords, and Eastern spices. Silk caps discovered in the Danelaw in northern England probably came from a roll of cloth imported from China by way of Byzantium.

In return, the Vikings exported many

valuable natural products found in Scandinavia. From Norway came soapstone (a soft stone that could be carved into cooking pots) and slate whetstones for sharpening tools and weapons.

Sweden exported high-quality iron ore, which was rare and precious. The ore could be used to make an iron breastplate, which might then be sold for the price of a dozen cows. Scandinavian amber, furs, antlers, and walrus tusks were also much in demand.

---

*Despite their love of battle, most Vikings are traders, not raiders. A majority spend their entire lives working peacefully as craftsmen or merchants.*

*In 960, Denmark's Hedeby is a bustling port, and its marketplace is crowded. Hedeby is particularly a center for trade in slaves captured in Russia and western Europe, but it offers many other goods, including jewelry, antlers, weapons, and luxuries from all over the world.*

# Hedeby

y the year 1000, many more Vikings lived in towns than on *bærs*, but even Hedeby, the largest Viking town, would seem small today. Judging by the number of graves left after 250 years of Viking occupation, archaeologists estimate that Hedeby was home to only about 1,000 people at any one time. Twice as many men as women lived in Hedeby, perhaps because the Vikings thought trade and craftwork were unsuitable occupations for women.

An Arab geographer who visited Hedeby reported that life was hard and the inhabitants poor. They lived mainly on fish, which was plentiful. Their main social activity took place on feast days, when people gathered together to honor their gods.

*The streets of Hedeby, a planned town, are laid out in a grid occupying about 10 acres (4 hectares) of land. Wooden planks cover them so they will not get muddy in the rain. The stream running through town has planked sides to prevent flooding.*

*Most houses are built of wattle and daub — willow branches threaded in and out of posts. Other buildings are made of horizontal planks fastened onto wooden stakes, or of rows of planks hammered vertically into the soil. The thralls and poor freemen live in a separate part of town, in damp sunken pits covered with thatched roofs.*

*The houses belonging to craftsmen and merchants are about 50 feet long by 20 feet wide (15 meters by 6) and face endways onto the street. Behind each house is a yard with a well, a cesspit for sewage, and a midden heap for garbage.*

*Before building a house, a Viking uses a yardstick to measure the site three times. If the second and third measurements are greater than the first, he believes, the ground is lucky and his wealth will increase.*

*The dyer who owns this house (center) hangs freshly dyed cloth in the yard to dry. A craftsman (left) tries to attract interest in the knives he has made.*

## In the Workshop

In towns like Hedeby there were many specialist craftspeople who made everything by hand in small workshops behind their houses. In such a town a Viking would find potters; coopers (barrel makers); cloth makers; tanners (leather workers); glass-bead specialists; locksmiths; soapstone carvers; bone carvers who fashioned ice skates, hairpins, coat toggles, and whorls (the weights used on a spinning wheel); and many other artisans.

Carpenters and carvers were perhaps the most important craftspeople. Carpenters made spoons and bowls, chests and chairs, and beds and benches, and they helped to build boats, houses, and churches. They decorated almost every surface with intricate carvings. A Viking carpenter did all this work himself, from felling the tree to polishing the finished product.

*While a customer buys a necklace, a Viking metalworker begins to hammer out a silver bracelet against an iron shoe inserted into a tree stump. The bracelet will go into a rich man's grave, and the beautifully decorated necklace (top), brooch (center), and ax (bottom) will go with it. Coins are rarely used and most trade is done by barter. When this is impossible, merchants use silver jewelry as currency.*

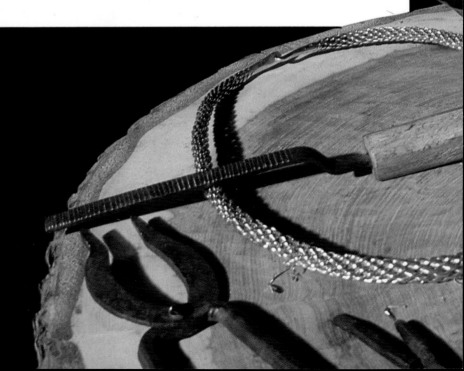

## The Coming of Christianity

The Catholic Church and the Christian kings of Europe continuously tried to convert the Vikings to their religion. They sent missionaries north, forbade Christians to trade with heathens, and sometimes made conversion of Viking raiders a condition of peace treaties. But the Vikings were not eager to give up their own gods. Some-

times Viking traders accepted a small cross meant to show that they were "interested" in Christianity — this allowed Christians to trade with them — but most Vikings did not convert until forced by their kings.

Olaf Tryggvason, who had been converted to Christianity while raiding in England, sought to convert his people, as well as those in Greenland and the Orkney Islands, when he became king of Norway in 995. At times Tryggvason was able to use

persuasion to convert people, but his methods were not always peaceful. He and his men sometimes broke into pagan temples and smashed the idols inside. At other times they threatened people who resisted conversion.

In the year 1000, Tryggvason demanded that Iceland, too, accept the new faith. After fierce debate in the Althing, Thorgeir, the *lögman*, suggested a compromise — Christianity would become the public religion, but people could make sacrifices to the Viking gods in private. Everyone agreed. A few years later, however, they lost even the right to sacrifice in private.

---

*Norwegian Vikings are tortured until they agree to accept Christianity. When Rauth, their leader, refuses to be converted, the king promises to put him to a hideous death. A hollow stick containing a snake will be forced between the victim's teeth. The snake will slide down into his stomach and eat its way out of his side, killing him slowly and painfully.*

# Times of Change

The kings who forced their people to accept Christianity were interested in more than spreading a religion: at the same time they were increasing their own power. Baptism often accompanied a ceremony in which a Viking promised to become "the king's man." While the power of the central government grew, the Things' influence declined.

Olaf Haraldsson, who ruled Norway after Olaf Tryggvason's death, continued to force people at Things all over the country to accept Christianity. If a Thing opposed him, Olaf often burned its entire district. Even jarls were not safe: Olaf put out several noblemen's eyes, and he cut off the tongue of a district ruler. Those who did accept Christianity had to hand over their sons as pledges of their faith. As long as the parents remained Christians, the sons remained alive. Eventually the jarls drove Olaf Haraldsson out of the country, letting Denmark's Cnut III take over.

In Sweden, Christianity was first established under the rule of Olaf Skottkonung, who came to power in 994 as the first king of the whole of Sweden. As in Norway, though, there was resistance, and the old beliefs survived for many years. As late as 1070 there was a great heathen revival led by a Viking known as Sacrifice Sven. It was only in 1100 that all the old temples were finally destroyed.

---

*Olaf Haraldsson, trying to regain power in Norway, is defeated and killed at the Battle of Stiklastad in 1030. Although Olaf loses his life he gains lasting fame. Later, miracles will be ascribed to him, and the Roman Catholic Church will make him a saint.*

# The End of the Viking Era

The Vikings were never united under one leader, yet for centuries they traveled, fought, and traded on four continents. Their world extended from America to Siberia and from the Arctic to the Mediterranean. Harald Hardrada, who became a king of Norway, fought in Scandinavia, England, Russia, and Byzantium. He was a man of international stature. Gudrid, one of the first female settlers in America, went on a pilgrimage to Rome; she was the most widely traveled woman in Europe in her time.

Nonetheless, the Vikings' power gradually declined. In Europe many states adopted the feudal system, giving local lords wealth and property in return for their services as calvary soldiers in the army. The Viking warriors were no match for these trained, heavily equipped soldiers. In 1066, at the Battle of Stamford Bridge, Harald Hardrada died trying to conquer England. In the same year, Polish tribesmen destroyed Hedeby. Vinland was abandoned and forgotten. The climate in Greenland grew colder, increasing the settlers' difficulties until, by 1410, the colony died out.

Although the power of the Vikings themselves declined in later years, many of their descendants — the Rus in Russia, the Normans in Normandy — continued to flourish. Even now, a thousand years after the Vikings, people still think some of their ideas about honor, law, democracy, women's equality, and individual freedom are important enough to fight for.

---

*It is 1066. A Norman knight surveys the land he gained as payment after the conquest of England. The Normans are direct descendants of the Vikings, who received Normandy from King Charles of France in 911.*

# How Do We Know?

The Vikings themselves did not write historical accounts of events as they unfolded. Historians must use indirect means of reconstructing what Viking life was like.

One way to find out about the Vikings is to read the books written by the people they attacked. In *The Frankish Annals,* French monks described the early raids on France and Germany. Viking armies also figure in *The Anglo-Saxon Chronicle,* a year-by-year historical account of the England of that time. These accounts, however, were written by the Vikings' enemies, who naturally were prejudiced against them. Therefore, the pictures these accounts give us may not be wholly accurate.

Emperor Constantine VII of Byzantium described the Rus in *The Book of Ceremonies,* which he wrote to give advice to his son. Both he and Ibn Fadlan, a Muslim writer, described Vikings whose customs had changed while they lived in Russia. In about 1070, Adam of Bremen's *Deeds of the Archbishops of Hamburg* described the Vikings in Scandinavia. But Adam was only writing down what other people had told him; he himself never visited the countries he wrote about.

## THE SAGAS

The Vikings passed on their laws, religion, customs, and history by word of mouth. They did record some information in runes on pieces of stone, wood, and bone, but it was not until about 1200, when the Vikings' descendants acquired paper and ink and began to write books, that the oral stories were extensively recorded.

The most famous Norse stories are *Egil's Saga, Njal's Saga,* and *The Saga of Olaf Tryggvason,* but dozens of others exist. In the 1220s, an Icelander called Snorri Sturluson collected many of them together in his book *The Heimskringla.* Although they tell stories about real people, the sagas cannot always be trusted. Their authors recorded events that had taken place 400 years earlier, and undoubtedly the sagas contain exaggerations and mistakes.

It is difficult to decide what to believe in these sagas. In *The Saga of Harald Hardrada,* for instance, Harald tricks a city into opening its gates by pretending he wants to bury one of his men inside. This story is similar to one about a Viking leader called Hastings, who lived about 200 years before Harald. Does this mean the writer of Harald's saga heard the story and decided to use it to make Harald look good? Or maybe Harald had heard the story and tried the same ruse. It is even possible that both men really did think up the same clever trick independently, but we will never know the truth.

## OTHER SOURCES

A few of the Vikings' achievements have survived the centuries intact. Large defensive mounds such as the Danevirke, built by the Viking kings of Denmark, still remain. In Sweden, some 12th-century wooden churches still stand. Rune stones found all over Scandinavia reveal a mass of small facts about the Vikings. European place names of Scandinavian origin show where the Vikings settled.

Archaeologists have dug up many other remains from Viking times. Some finds, such as the Swedish treasure hoards and the Gokstad ship, have been very exciting. Graves, especially those containing personal possessions, reveal a lot about the lives and

beliefs of the occupants. Other excavations, such as those at Hedeby in Denmark and Jorvik (York) in England, have shown us a great deal about the lives of ordinary people. Analyzing a piece of human excrement can tell a lot about a Viking's diet, for instance, and the scratches on the bottom of a ship can show us how it was used.

FINDING THE ANSWERS

Occasionally, archaeologists are able to link their findings to the stories in the sagas. *The Saga of Eric the Red,* for example, tells how Thorvald, the brother of Leif the Lucky, led an expedition to a country west of Greenland, where Skrælings killed him. Because of this story, some historians suspected that the Vikings had reached America, but by itself the evidence in the sagas did not prove that Vinland really was North America. *The Saga of Eric the Red* was not written until about 1225, long after the events it re-

ported took place. A "Viking" map showing North America was found in Germany but turned out to have been drawn with a kind of ink that was only available in the 20th century.

For many years, historians suspected the saga writers had made up these stories. Then archaeologists found a Native American arrowhead on Gudrid's farm in Greenland. They also found Viking coffins made from larch and maple trees, which, during the Viking age, grew only in North America. Finally, in the 1960s, historians unearthed an ancient settlement in Newfoundland, Canada. The village included a hall with banks of earth along the walls in typical Viking style, a soapstone spinning-whorl, and an iron nail—though Native Americans did not work metal at the time the house was built. This find proved beyond doubt that the Vikings sailed to America and settled there for some time.

Still, there are some questions without answers. The Jomsvikings' fortress, for instance, has never been found. Is this because it never existed, because it was destroyed, or because it was obliterated by later building? Maybe, one day, a team of archaeologists will discover the answer. Perhaps, with luck and hard work, you will be a member of that team.

# Index

800 AD    850 AD    900 AD    950 AD

*800–814* Charlemagne,
Holy Roman Emperor

*January 878* Vikings defeated
by the English at the
Battle of the Raven

*c.800* Viking raids
on Europe begin
to increase

*May 878* Guthrum,
ruler of the Danelaw,
baptized as a Christian

*c.800* Russian traders
travel down the Dneiper River

*911* King Charles of France
gives Normandy to Rolo the Fat

*c.808* Godfred, King of
Denmark, attacks Reric, moves
craftsmen to Hedeby

*844* The Vikings
conquer islands off
the coast of France

*922* Ibn Fadlan meets the
Rus on the River Volga

*851* Viking raiders
spend their first winter
in England

*860* Iceland
discovered

*865–895* The Great Heathen Host
ravages England, France, and Belgium.
The Danelaw is established

Norw

of gold fr

*986* Er
leads a colon
to G

*990* Batt
Norwegian

*991*

*874* The first colonizing
expedition to Iceland

becom
tries to co

be
beg

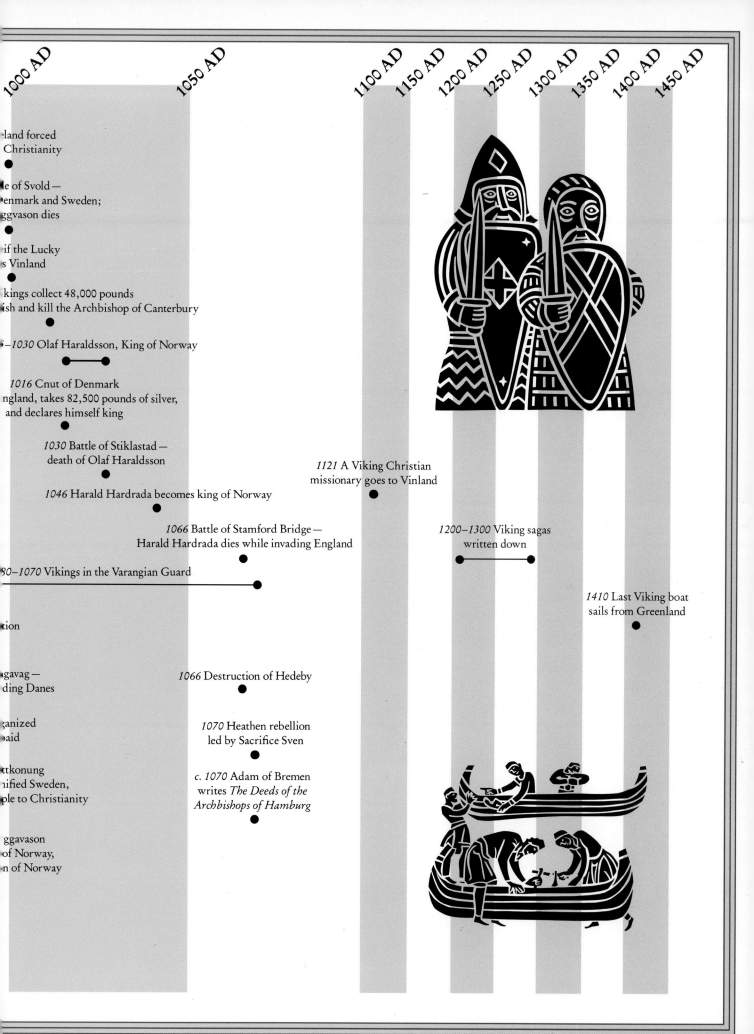

1000 AD       1050 AD       1100 AD   1150 AD   1200 AD   1250 AD   1300 AD   1350 AD   1400 AD   1450 AD

eland forced
Christianity

e of Svold —
enmark and Sweden;
ggvason dies

if the Lucky
s Vinland

kings collect 48,000 pounds
ish and kill the Archbishop of Canterbury

—1030 Olaf Haraldsson, King of Norway

*1016* Cnut of Denmark
ngland, takes 82,500 pounds of silver,
and declares himself king

*1030* Battle of Stiklastad —
death of Olaf Haraldsson

*1121* A Viking Christian
missionary goes to Vinland

*1046* Harald Hardrada becomes king of Norway

*1200–1300* Viking sagas
written down

*1066* Battle of Stamford Bridge —
Harald Hardrada dies while invading England

*1410* Last Viking boat
sails from Greenland

80–1070 Vikings in the Varangian Guard

tion

gavag —
ding Danes

*1066* Destruction of Hedeby

ganized
aid

*1070* Heathen rebellion
led by Sacrifice Sven

ttkonung
nified Sweden,
ple to Christianity

*c. 1070* Adam of Bremen
writes *The Deeds of the
Archbishops of Hamburg*

ggavason
of Norway,
n of Norway